Pebble Plus

Special Diets

Diabetes-Aware Diets

by Mari Schuh

Consulting Editor: Gail Saunders-Smith, PhD

Consultant:
Amy L. Lusk, MS, RD, LD, CDE
Registered Dietitian

CAPSTONE PRESS
a capstone imprint

Pebble Plus is published by Capstone Press,
1710 Roe Crest Drive, North Mankato, Minnesota 56003.
www.capstonepub.com

Library of Congress Cataloging-in-Publication Data
Schuh, Mari C., 1975– author.
Diabetes-aware diets / by Mari Schuh
pages cm. — (Pebble plus. Special diets)
Audience: Age 4-8.
Audience: Grades K to 3.
Includes bibliographical references and index.
ISBN 978-1-4914-0592-5 (library binding: alk. paper)
ISBN 978-1-4914-6585-1 (paperback)
ISBN 978-1-4914-0626-7 (eBook pdf)
1. Diabetes—Juvenile literature. 2. Diabetes—Diet therapy—Juvenile literature.
I. Title
RC660.5.S38 2015
616.4'62—dc23   2013050810
2011049857

Editorial Credits
Shelly Lyons, editor; Heidi Thompson, designer; Kelly Garvin, media researcher;
    Katy LaVigne, production specialist

Photo Credits
All photos by Capstone Studios/Karon Dubke

Note to Parents and Teachers

The Special Diets series supports national science standards related to health and nutrition.
This book describes and illustrates some foods that fit and don't fit into a diabetes-aware diet.
The images support early readers in understanding the text. The repetition of words and phrases
helps early readers learn new words. This book also introduces early readers to subject-specific
vocabulary words, which are defined in the Glossary section. Early readers may need assistance
to read some words and to use the Table of Contents, Glossary, Read More, Internet Sites, and
Index sections of the book.

Printed in the United States   4315

Table of Contents

Who Needs a Diabetes-Aware Diet?

A person's body normally

turns food into fuel for itself.

If someone has diabetes,

the body has trouble doing this.

Someone with diabetes may need
to eat at certain times each day.
She also might need to plan
meals and snacks.

Eat This, Not That

People with diabetes

may eat balanced meals.

Vegetables cover half the plate.

Some meat, bread,

and fruit is added.

Small portions may be important

for someone with diabetes.

A few cups of popcorn

make a great snack.

Like others, people with diabetes
can eat some sweets.
They might enjoy
a sugar-free frozen treat.

Instead of cookies
a bit of nuts or cheese
is a healthier choice.

What Happens to People with Diabetes?

People with diabetes must test

their blood sugar level.

If the level is too high or low,

they can become ill.

Someone with diabetes
might seem confused.
She may shake or sweat.
Tell an adult and call 911.

Be a Good Friend

Some people with diabetes

wear a medical ID bracelet.

They may need medicine every day.

They want friends who understand.

You can be a good friend!

Safe Recipe
Layered Lunch Wrap

What You Need

2 tbsp. (30 mL) low-fat plain yogurt
        or Greek yogurt
1 whole-wheat tortilla
1 oz. (30 grams) turkey, sliced thin
1 oz. (30 grams) ham, sliced thin
1 oz. (30 grams) Swiss cheese slice
2-3 fresh spinach leaves
¼ cup (60 mL) chopped tomato
¼ cup (60 mL) chopped cucumber
plastic wrap

What You Do

Ask an adult to help you. Spread the yogurt
on one side of the tortilla. Layer the turkey, ham,
cheese, and spinach on the yogurt. Add the chopped
tomatoes and cucumbers. Fold in the top and bottom edges
of the tortilla. Roll up the sides to form a tube. Wrap in plastic
wrap until ready to eat.

Makes 1 wrap
Diabetes Exchanges: 2 exchanges equals
30 grams of carbohydrates

Glossary

blood sugar—the amount of glucose, or sugar, in our blood

fuel—a source of energy

medical ID bracelet—a bracelet that a person wears to tell others about a medical problem

portion—a certain amount of food

Read More

Bryan, Jenny. *I Have Diabetes*. Taking Care of Myself. New York: Gareth Stevens Pub., 2011.

Parker, Vic. *I Know Someone with Diabetes*. Understanding Health Issues. Chicago: Heinemann Library, 2011.

Robbins, Lynette. *How to Deal with Diabetes*. Kids' Health. New York: PowerKids Press, 2010.

Internet Sites

FactHound offers a safe, fun way to find Internet sites related to this book. All of the sites on FactHound have been researched by our staff.

Here's all you do:
Visit *www.facthound.com*
Type in this code: 9781491405925

Check out projects, games and lots more at **www.capstonekids.com**

Index

Critical Thinking Using the Common Core

1. Healthy foods are an important part of a diabetes-aware diet. What are some healthy foods that you can include in your diet? (Key Ideas and Details)

2. What are some signs that a person with diabetes may need medical help? (Key Ideas and Details)

Word Count: 172
Grade: 1
Early-Intervention Level: 16